This planner belongs to :

_____

2026

January

S	M	T	W	T	F	S
				1	2	3
4	5	6	7	8	9	10
11	12	13	14	15	16	17
18	19	20	21	22	23	24
25	26	27	28	29	30	31

February

S	M	T	W	T	F	S
1	2	3	4	5	6	7
8	9	10	11	12	13	14
15	16	17	18	19	20	21
22	23	24	25	26	27	28

March

S	M	T	W	T	F	S
1	2	3	4	5	6	7
8	9	10	11	12	13	14
15	16	17	18	19	20	21
22	23	24	25	26	27	28
29	30	31				

April

S	M	T	W	T	F	S
			1	2	3	4
5	6	7	8	9	10	11
12	13	14	15	16	17	18
19	20	21	22	23	24	25
26	27	28	29	30		

May

S	M	T	W	T	F	S
					1	2
3	4	5	6	7	8	9
10	11	12	13	14	15	16
17	18	19	20	21	22	23
24	25	26	27	28	29	30
31						

June

S	M	T	W	T	F	S
	1	2	3	4	5	6
7	8	9	10	11	12	13
14	15	16	17	18	19	20
21	22	23	24	25	26	27
28	29	30				

July

S	M	T	W	T	F	S
			1	2	3	4
5	6	7	8	9	10	11
12	13	14	15	16	17	18
19	20	21	22	23	24	25
26	27	28	29	30	31	

August

S	M	T	W	T	F	S
						1
2	3	4	5	6	7	8
9	10	11	12	13	14	15
16	17	18	19	20	21	22
23	24	25	26	27	28	29
30	31					

September

S	M	T	W	T	F	S
		1	2	3	4	5
6	7	8	9	10	11	12
13	14	15	16	17	18	19
20	21	22	23	24	25	26
27	28	29	30			

October

S	M	T	W	T	F	S
				1	2	3
4	5	6	7	8	9	10
11	12	13	14	15	16	17
18	19	20	21	22	23	24
25	26	27	28	29	30	31

November

S	M	T	W	T	F	S
1	2	3	4	5	6	7
8	9	10	11	12	13	14
15	16	17	18	19	20	21
22	23	24	25	26	27	28
29	30					

December

S	M	T	W	T	F	S
		1	2	3	4	5
6	7	8	9	10	11	12
13	14	15	16	17	18	19
20	21	22	23	24	25	26
27	28	29	30	31		

Year in Pixels

	J	F	M	A	M	J	J	A	S	O	N	D
1.												
2.												
3.												
4.												
5.												
6.												
7.												
8.												
9.												
10.												
11.												
12.												
13.												
14.												
15.												
16.												
17.												
18.												
19.												
20.												
21.												
22.												
23.												
24.												
25.												
26.												
27.												
28.												
29.												
30.												
31.												

Color Codes

Notes

January

2026

MONDAY	TUESDAY	WEDNESDAY	THURSDAY
			1
5	6	7	8
12	13	14	15
19	20	21	22
26	27	28	29

January

FRIDAY	SATURDAY	SUNDAY	NOTES
2	3	4	○
			○
			○
			○
			○
9	10	11	○
			○
			○
			○
			○
16	17	18	○
			○
			○
			○
			○
23	24	25	○
			○
			○
			○
			○
30	31		NOTES

February

MONDAY	TUESDAY	WEDNESDAY	THURSDAY
2	3	4	5
9	10	11	12
16	17	18	19
23	24	25	26

February

FRIDAY	SATURDAY	SUNDAY	NOTES
		1	○
			○
			○
			○
			○
6	7	8	○
			○
			○
			○
13	14	15	○
			○
			○
			○
			○
20	21	22	○
			○
			○
			○
			○
27	28		NOTES

March 2026

MONDAY	TUESDAY	WEDNESDAY	THURSDAY
2	3	4	5
9	10	11	12
16	17	18	19
23	24	25	26

March 2026

FRIDAY	SATURDAY	SUNDAY	NOTES
		1	○
			○
			○
			○
			○
6	7	8	○
			○
			○
			○
			○
13	14	15	○
			○
			○
			○
			○
20	21	22	○
			○
			○
			○
			○
27	28	29	30
			31

April 2026

MONDAY	TUESDAY	WEDNESDAY	THURSDAY
		1	2
6	7	8	9
13	14	15	16
20	21	22	23
27	28	29	30

April

FRIDAY	SATURDAY	SUNDAY	NOTES
3	4	5	○
			○
			○
			○
			○
10	11	12	○
			○
			○
			○
17	18	19	○
			○
			○
			○
			○
24	25	26	○
			○
			○
			○
			○
			NOTES

May

MONDAY	TUESDAY	WEDNESDAY	THURSDAY
4	5	6	7
11	12	13	14
18	19	20	21
25	26	27	28

May

2026

FRIDAY	SATURDAY	SUNDAY	NOTES
1	2	3	○
			○
			○
			○
			○
8	9	10	○
			○
			○
			○
15	16	17	○
			○
			○
			○
			○
22	23	24	○
			○
			○
			○
			○
29	30	31	Notes

June

MONDAY	TUESDAY	WEDNESDAY	THURSDAY
1	2	3	4
8	9	10	11
15	16	17	18
22	23	24	25
29	30		

June

2026

FRIDAY	SATURDAY	SUNDAY	NOTES
5	6	7	○
			○
			○
			○
			○
12	13	14	○
			○
			○
			○
19	20	21	○
			○
			○
			○
			○
26	27	28	○
			○
			○
			○
			○
			Notes

July

2026

MONDAY	TUESDAY	WEDNESDAY	THURSDAY
		1	2
6	7	8	9
13	14	15	16
20	21	22	23
27	28	29	30

July

FRIDAY	SATURDAY	SUNDAY	NOTES
3	4	5	○
			○
			○
			○
			○
10	11	12	○
			○
			○
			○
17	18	19	○
			○
			○
			○
			○
24	25	26	○
			○
			○
			○
			○
31			NOTES

August

MONDAY	TUESDAY	WEDNESDAY	THURSDAY
3	4	5	6
10	11	12	13
17	18	19	20
24	25	26	27

August 2026

FRIDAY	SATURDAY	SUNDAY	NOTES
	1	2	○
			○
			○
			○
			○
7	8	9	○
			○
			○
			○
14	15	16	○
			○
			○
			○
			○
21	22	23	○
			○
			○
			○
			○
28	29	30	31

September

MONDAY	TUESDAY	WEDNESDAY	THURSDAY
	1	2	3
7	8	9	10
14	15	16	17
21	22	23	24
28	29	30	

September 2026

FRIDAY	SATURDAY	SUNDAY	NOTES
4	5	6	○
			○
			○
			○
			○
11	12	13	○
			○
			○
			○
18	19	20	○
			○
			○
			○
			○
25	26	27	○
			○
			○
			○
			○
			NOTES

October 2026

MONDAY	TUESDAY	WEDNESDAY	THURSDAY
			1
5	6	7	8
12	13	14	15
19	20	21	22
26	27	28	29

October  2026

FRIDAY	SATURDAY	SUNDAY	NOTES
2	3	4	○
			○
			○
			○
9	10	11	○
			○
			○
			○
			○
16	17	18	○
			○
			○
			○
			○
23	24	25	○
			○
			○
			○
			○
30	31		NOTES

November 2026

MONDAY	TUESDAY	WEDNESDAY	THURSDAY
2	3	4	5
9	10	11	12
16	17	18	19
23	24	25	26

November   2026

FRIDAY	SATURDAY	SUNDAY	NOTES
		1	○
			○
			○
			○
			○
6	7	8	○
			○
			○
			○
13	14	15	○
			○
			○
			○
			○
20	21	22	○
			○
			○
			○
			○
27	28	29	30

December

MONDAY	TUESDAY	WEDNESDAY	THURSDAY
	1	2	3
7	8	9	10
14	15	16	17
21	22	23	24
28	29	30	31

December

2026

FRIDAY	SATURDAY	SUNDAY	NOTES
4	5	6	○
			○
			○
			○
			○
11	12	13	○
			○
			○
			○
18	19	20	○
			○
			○
			○
			○
25	26	27	○
			○
			○
			○
			○
			NOTES

December
2025

01 MONDAY

02 TUESDAY

03 WEDNESDAY

04 FRIDAY

December
2025

05 FRIDAY

06 SATURDAY

07 SUNDAY

08 MONDAY

09 TUESDAY

10 WEDNESDAY

11 THURSDAY

12 FRIDAY

13 SATURDAY

14 SUNDAY

15 MONDAY

16 TUESDAY

17 WEDNESDAY

18 THURSDAY

19 FRIDAY

20 SATURDAY

21 SUNDAY

22 MONDAY

23 TUESDAY

24 WEDNESDAY

25 THURSDAY

○
○
○
○
○
○
○
○

26 FRIDAY

○
○
○
○
○
○
○
○

27 SATURDAY

○
○
○
○
○
○
○
○

28 SUNDAY

○
○
○
○
○

December
2025

29 MONDAY

○ _____
○ _____
○ _____
○ _____
○ _____
○ _____
○ _____
○ _____

30 TUESDAY

○ _____
○ _____
○ _____
○ _____
○ _____
○ _____
○ _____
○ _____

31 WEDNESDAY

○ _____
○ _____
○ _____
○ _____
○ _____
○ _____
○ _____
○ _____

NOTES

_____
_____
_____
_____

January
2026

01 THURSDAY

○
○
○
○
○
○
○

02 FRIDAY

○
○
○
○
○
○
○
○

03 SATURDAY

○
○
○
○
○
○
○
○

04 SUNDAY

○
○
○
○

05 MONDAY

○ _____
○ _____
○ _____
○ _____
○ _____
○ _____
○ _____
○ _____

06 TUESDAY

○ _____
○ _____
○ _____
○ _____
○ _____
○ _____
○ _____
○ _____

07 WEDNESDAY

○ _____
○ _____
○ _____
○ _____
○ _____
○ _____
○ _____
○ _____

08 THURSDAY

○ _____
○ _____
○ _____
○ _____
○ _____

January
2026

09 FRIDAY
- ○
- ○
- ○
- ○
- ○
- ○
- ○
- ○

10 SATURDAY
- ○
- ○
- ○
- ○
- ○
- ○
- ○
- ○

11 SUNDAY
- ○
- ○
- ○
- ○
- ○
- ○
- ○
- ○

12 MONDAY
- ○
- ○
- ○
- ○
- ○

13 TUESDAY

○
○
○
○
○
○
○
○

14 WEDNESDAY

○
○
○
○
○
○
○
○

15 THURSDAY

○
○
○
○
○
○
○
○

16 FRIDAY

○
○
○
○
○

17 SATURDAY

○ _____
○ _____
○ _____
○ _____
○ _____
○ _____
○ _____
○ _____

18 SUNDAY

○ _____
○ _____
○ _____
○ _____
○ _____
○ _____
○ _____
○ _____

19 MONDAY

○ _____
○ _____
○ _____
○ _____
○ _____
○ _____
○ _____
○ _____

20 TUESDAY

○ _____
○ _____
○ _____
○ _____

21 WEDNESDAY

22 THURSDAY

23 FRIDAY

24 SATURDAY

25 SUNDAY
○
○
○
○
○
○
○

26 MONDAY
○
○
○
○
○
○
○
○

27 TUESDAY
○
○
○
○
○
○
○
○

28 WEDNESDAY
○
○
○
○

29 THURSDAY

○ _____
○ _____
○ _____
○ _____
○ _____
○ _____
○ _____
○ _____

30 FRIDAY

○ _____
○ _____
○ _____
○ _____
○ _____
○ _____
○ _____
○ _____

31 SATURDAY

○ _____
○ _____
○ _____
○ _____
○ _____
○ _____
○ _____
○ _____

NOTES

_____
_____
_____
_____

February
2026

01 SUNDAY
- ○ _____
- ○ _____
- ○ _____
- ○ _____
- ○ _____
- ○ _____
- ○ _____
- ○ _____

02 MONDAY
- ○ _____
- ○ _____
- ○ _____
- ○ _____
- ○ _____
- ○ _____
- ○ _____
- ○ _____

03 TUESDAY
- ○ _____
- ○ _____
- ○ _____
- ○ _____
- ○ _____
- ○ _____
- ○ _____
- ○ _____

04 WEDNESDAY
- ○ _____
- ○ _____
- ○ _____
- ○ _____
- ○ _____

February
2026

05 THURSDAY
○
○
○
○
○
○
○
○

06 FRIDAY
○
○
○
○
○
○
○
○

07 SATURDAY
○
○
○
○
○
○
○
○

08 SUNDAY
○
○
○
○
○

February
2026

09 MONDAY

○
○
○
○
○
○
○
○

10 TUESDAY

○
○
○
○
○
○
○
○

11 WEDNESDAY

○
○
○
○
○
○
○
○

12 THURSDAY

○
○
○
○

February
2026

13 FRIDAY

○
○
○
○
○
○
○
○

14 SATURDAY

○
○
○
○
○
○
○
○

15 SUNDAY

○
○
○
○
○
○
○
○

16 MONDAY

○
○
○
○
○

17 TUESDAY

○
○
○
○
○
○
○
○

18 WEDNESDAY

○
○
○
○
○
○
○
○

19 THURSDAY

○
○
○
○
○
○
○
○

20 FRIDAY

○
○
○
○

February
2026

21 SATURDAY

○ _____
○ _____
○ _____
○ _____
○ _____
○ _____
○ _____
○ _____

22 SUNDAY

○ _____
○ _____
○ _____
○ _____
○ _____
○ _____
○ _____
○ _____

23 MONDAY

○ _____
○ _____
○ _____
○ _____
○ _____
○ _____
○ _____
○ _____

24 TUESDAY

○ _____
○ _____
○ _____
○ _____
○ _____

February
2026

25 WEDNESDAY

26 THURSDAY

27 FRIDAY

28 SATURDAY

March
2026

01 SUNDAY

○ _____
○ _____
○ _____
○ _____
○ _____
○ _____
○ _____
○ _____

02 MONDAY

○ _____
○ _____
○ _____
○ _____
○ _____
○ _____
○ _____
○ _____

03 TUESDAY

○ _____
○ _____
○ _____
○ _____
○ _____
○ _____
○ _____
○ _____

04 WEDNESDAY

○ _____
○ _____
○ _____
○ _____
○ _____

March
2026

05 THURSDAY

06 FRIDAY

07 SATURDAY

08 SUNDAY

March
2026

09 MONDAY

○ ──────────────────────────
○ ──────────────────────────
○ ──────────────────────────
○ ──────────────────────────
○ ──────────────────────────
○ ──────────────────────────
○ ──────────────────────────
○ ──────────────────────────

10 TUESDAY

○ ──────────────────────────
○ ──────────────────────────
○ ──────────────────────────
○ ──────────────────────────
○ ──────────────────────────
○ ──────────────────────────
○ ──────────────────────────
○ ──────────────────────────

11 WEDNESDAY

○ ──────────────────────────
○ ──────────────────────────
○ ──────────────────────────
○ ──────────────────────────
○ ──────────────────────────
○ ──────────────────────────
○ ──────────────────────────
○ ──────────────────────────

12 THURSDAY

○ ──────────────────────────
○ ──────────────────────────
○ ──────────────────────────
○ ──────────────────────────
○ ──────────────────────────

13 FRIDAY

○
○
○
○
○
○
○
○

14 SATURDAY

○
○
○
○
○
○
○
○

15 SUNDAY

○
○
○
○
○
○
○
○

16 MONDAY

○
○
○
○

17 TUESDAY

○ _____
○ _____
○ _____
○ _____
○ _____
○ _____
○ _____
○ _____

18 WEDNESDAY

○ _____
○ _____
○ _____
○ _____
○ _____
○ _____
○ _____
○ _____

19 THURSDAY

○ _____
○ _____
○ _____
○ _____
○ _____
○ _____
○ _____
○ _____

20 FRIDAY

○ _____
○ _____
○ _____
○ _____
○ _____

21 SATURDAY

○
○
○
○
○
○
○
○

22 SUNDAY

○
○
○
○
○
○
○
○

23 MONDAY

○
○
○
○
○
○
○
○

24 TUESDAY

○
○
○
○

March
2026

25 WEDNESDAY

○ _____
○ _____
○ _____
○ _____
○ _____
○ _____
○ _____
○ _____

26 THURSDAY

○ _____
○ _____
○ _____
○ _____
○ _____
○ _____
○ _____
○ _____

27 FRIDAY

○ _____
○ _____
○ _____
○ _____
○ _____
○ _____
○ _____
○ _____

28 SATURDAY

○ _____
○ _____
○ _____
○ _____
○ _____

March
2026

29 SUNDAY

○ _____
○ _____
○ _____
○ _____
○ _____
○ _____
○ _____
○ _____

30 MONDAY

○ _____
○ _____
○ _____
○ _____
○ _____
○ _____
○ _____
○ _____

31 TUESDAY

○ _____
○ _____
○ _____
○ _____
○ _____
○ _____
○ _____

NOTES

_____
_____
_____
_____
_____

April
2026

01 WEDNESDAY
- ○
- ○
- ○
- ○
- ○
- ○
- ○
- ○

02 THURSDAY
- ○
- ○
- ○
- ○
- ○
- ○
- ○
- ○

03 FRIDAY
- ○
- ○
- ○
- ○
- ○
- ○
- ○
- ○

04 SATURDAY
- ○
- ○
- ○
- ○
- ○

April
2026

05 SUNDAY

06 MONDAY

07 TUESDAY

08 WEDNESDAY

April
2026

09 THURSDAY

○ _____
○ _____
○ _____
○ _____
○ _____
○ _____
○ _____
○ _____

10 FRIDAY

○ _____
○ _____
○ _____
○ _____
○ _____
○ _____
○ _____
○ _____

11 SATURDAY

○ _____
○ _____
○ _____
○ _____
○ _____
○ _____
○ _____
○ _____

12 SUNDAY

○ _____
○ _____
○ _____
○ _____
○ _____

13 MONDAY

14 TUESDAY

15 WEDNESDAY

16 THURSDAY

April
2026

17 FRIDAY

○ _____
○ _____
○ _____
○ _____
○ _____
○ _____
○ _____
○ _____

18 SATURDAY

○ _____
○ _____
○ _____
○ _____
○ _____
○ _____
○ _____
○ _____

19 SUNDAY

○ _____
○ _____
○ _____
○ _____
○ _____
○ _____
○ _____
○ _____

20 MONDAY

○ _____
○ _____
○ _____
○ _____
○ _____

21 TUESDAY

22 WEDNESDAY

23 THURSDAY

24 FRIDAY

April
2026

25 SATURDAY

○ _____
○ _____
○ _____
○ _____
○ _____
○ _____
○ _____
○ _____

26 SUNDAY

○ _____
○ _____
○ _____
○ _____
○ _____
○ _____
○ _____
○ _____

27 MONDAY

○ _____
○ _____
○ _____
○ _____
○ _____
○ _____
○ _____
○ _____

28 TUESDAY

○ _____
○ _____
○ _____
○ _____
○ _____

29 WEDNESDAY

○ _____
○ _____
○ _____
○ _____
○ _____
○ _____
○ _____
○ _____

30 THURSDAY

○ _____
○ _____
○ _____
○ _____
○ _____
○ _____
○ _____
○ _____

NOTES

_____
_____
_____
_____
_____
_____
_____
_____
_____
_____
_____
_____
_____

April
2026

25 SATURDAY

○ _____
○ _____
○ _____
○ _____
○ _____
○ _____
○ _____
○ _____

26 SUNDAY

○ _____
○ _____
○ _____
○ _____
○ _____
○ _____
○ _____
○ _____

27 MONDAY

○ _____
○ _____
○ _____
○ _____
○ _____
○ _____
○ _____
○ _____

28 TUESDAY

○ _____
○ _____
○ _____
○ _____
○ _____

April
2026

29 WEDNESDAY

- ○ _____
- ○ _____
- ○ _____
- ○ _____
- ○ _____
- ○ _____
- ○ _____
- ○ _____

30 THURSDAY

- ○ _____
- ○ _____
- ○ _____
- ○ _____
- ○ _____
- ○ _____
- ○ _____
- ○ _____

NOTES

May
2026

01 FRIDAY
- ○ _____
- ○ _____
- ○ _____
- ○ _____
- ○ _____
- ○ _____
- ○ _____
- ○ _____

02 SATURDAY
- ○ _____
- ○ _____
- ○ _____
- ○ _____
- ○ _____
- ○ _____
- ○ _____
- ○ _____

03 SUNDAY
- ○ _____
- ○ _____
- ○ _____
- ○ _____
- ○ _____
- ○ _____
- ○ _____
- ○ _____

04 MONDAY
- ○ _____
- ○ _____
- ○ _____
- ○ _____
- ○ _____

May
2026

05 TUESDAY

○
○
○
○
○
○
○
○

06 WEDNESDAY

○
○
○
○
○
○
○
○

07 THURSDAY

○
○
○
○
○
○
○
○

08 FRIDAY

○
○
○
○
○

May
2026

09 SATURDAY

10 SUNDAY

11 MONDAY

12 TUESDAY

13 WEDNESDAY

- ○
- ○
- ○
- ○
- ○
- ○
- ○
- ○

14 THURSDAY

- ○
- ○
- ○
- ○
- ○
- ○
- ○
- ○

15 FRIDAY

- ○
- ○
- ○
- ○
- ○
- ○
- ○
- ○

16 SATURDAY

- ○
- ○
- ○
- ○
- ○

May
2026

17 SUNDAY
- ○
- ○
- ○
- ○
- ○
- ○
- ○
- ○

18 MONDAY
- ○
- ○
- ○
- ○
- ○
- ○
- ○
- ○

19 TUESDAY
- ○
- ○
- ○
- ○
- ○
- ○
- ○
- ○

20 WEDNESDAY
- ○
- ○
- ○
- ○
- ○

May
2026

21 THURSDAY

○ _____
○ _____
○ _____
○ _____
○ _____
○ _____
○ _____
○ _____

22 FRIDAY

○ _____
○ _____
○ _____
○ _____
○ _____
○ _____
○ _____
○ _____

23 SATURDAY

○ _____
○ _____
○ _____
○ _____
○ _____
○ _____
○ _____
○ _____

24 SUNDAY

○ _____
○ _____
○ _____
○ _____
○ _____

25 MONDAY
- ○
- ○
- ○
- ○
- ○
- ○
- ○
- ○

26 TUESDAY
- ○
- ○
- ○
- ○
- ○
- ○
- ○
- ○

27 WEDNESDAY
- ○
- ○
- ○
- ○
- ○
- ○
- ○
- ○

28 THURSDAY
- ○
- ○
- ○
- ○
- ○

May
2026

29 FRIDAY
○ _____
○ _____
○ _____
○ _____
○ _____
○ _____
○ _____
○ _____

30 SATURDAY
○ _____
○ _____
○ _____
○ _____
○ _____
○ _____
○ _____
○ _____

31 SUNDAY
○ _____
○ _____
○ _____
○ _____
○ _____
○ _____
○ _____
○ _____

NOTES
_____
_____
_____
_____

June 2026

01 MONDAY

○ _____
○ _____
○ _____
○ _____
○ _____
○ _____
○ _____
○ _____

02 TUESDAY

○ _____
○ _____
○ _____
○ _____
○ _____
○ _____
○ _____
○ _____

03 WEDNESDAY

○ _____
○ _____
○ _____
○ _____
○ _____
○ _____
○ _____
○ _____

04 THURSDAY

○ _____
○ _____
○ _____
○ _____
○ _____

June 2026

05 FRIDAY

○
○
○
○
○
○
○
○

06 SATURDAY

○
○
○
○
○
○
○
○

07 SUNDAY

○
○
○
○
○
○
○
○

08 MONDAY

○
○
○
○
○

09 TUESDAY

○ _____
○ _____
○ _____
○ _____
○ _____
○ _____
○ _____
○ _____

10 WEDNESDAY

○ _____
○ _____
○ _____
○ _____
○ _____
○ _____
○ _____
○ _____

11 THURSDAY

○ _____
○ _____
○ _____
○ _____
○ _____
○ _____
○ _____
○ _____

12 FRIDAY

○ _____
○ _____
○ _____
○ _____
○ _____

13 SATURDAY

14 SUNDAY

15 MONDAY

16 TUESDAY

17 WEDNESDAY

○ _____
○ _____
○ _____
○ _____
○ _____
○ _____
○ _____
○ _____

18 THURSDAY

○ _____
○ _____
○ _____
○ _____
○ _____
○ _____
○ _____
○ _____

19 FRIDAY

○ _____
○ _____
○ _____
○ _____
○ _____
○ _____
○ _____
○ _____

20 SATURDAY

○ _____
○ _____
○ _____
○ _____
○ _____

21 SUNDAY

22 MONDAY

23 TUESDAY

24 WEDNESDAY

25 THURSDAY
- ○ _____
- ○ _____
- ○ _____
- ○ _____
- ○ _____
- ○ _____
- ○ _____
- ○ _____

26 FRIDAY
- ○ _____
- ○ _____
- ○ _____
- ○ _____
- ○ _____
- ○ _____
- ○ _____
- ○ _____

27 SATURDAY
- ○ _____
- ○ _____
- ○ _____
- ○ _____
- ○ _____
- ○ _____
- ○ _____
- ○ _____

28 SUNDAY
- ○ _____
- ○ _____
- ○ _____
- ○ _____
- ○ _____

June
2026

29 MONDAY

○ _____
○ _____
○ _____
○ _____
○ _____
○ _____
○ _____
○ _____

30 TUESDAY

○ _____
○ _____
○ _____
○ _____
○ _____
○ _____
○ _____
○ _____

NOTES

_____
_____
_____
_____
_____
_____
_____
_____
_____
_____
_____
_____

01 WEDNESDAY

- ○
- ○
- ○
- ○
- ○
- ○
- ○
- ○

02 THURSDAY

- ○
- ○
- ○
- ○
- ○
- ○
- ○
- ○

03 FRIDAY

- ○
- ○
- ○
- ○
- ○
- ○
- ○
- ○

04 SATURDAY

- ○
- ○
- ○
- ○
- ○

05 SUNDAY
- ○
- ○
- ○
- ○
- ○
- ○
- ○
- ○

06 MONDAY
- ○
- ○
- ○
- ○
- ○
- ○
- ○
- ○

07 TUESDAY
- ○
- ○
- ○
- ○
- ○
- ○
- ○
- ○

08 WEDNESDAY
- ○
- ○
- ○
- ○
- ○

July
2026

09 THURSDAY

○ _____
○ _____
○ _____
○ _____
○ _____
○ _____
○ _____
○ _____

10 FRIDAY

○ _____
○ _____
○ _____
○ _____
○ _____
○ _____
○ _____
○ _____

11 SATURDAY

○ _____
○ _____
○ _____
○ _____
○ _____
○ _____
○ _____
○ _____

12 SUNDAY

○ _____
○ _____
○ _____
○ _____
○ _____

13 MONDAY

14 TUESDAY

15 WEDNESDAY

16 THURSDAY

17 FRIDAY

○ _____
○ _____
○ _____
○ _____
○ _____
○ _____
○ _____
○ _____

18 SATURDAY

○ _____
○ _____
○ _____
○ _____
○ _____
○ _____
○ _____
○ _____

19 SUNDAY

○ _____
○ _____
○ _____
○ _____
○ _____
○ _____
○ _____
○ _____

20 MONDAY

○ _____
○ _____
○ _____
○ _____
○ _____

21 TUESDAY

○
_____
○
_____
○
_____
○
_____
○
_____
○
_____
○
_____
○
_____

22 WEDNESDAY

○
_____
○
_____
○
_____
○
_____
○
_____
○
_____
○
_____
○
_____

23 THURSDAY

○
_____
○
_____
○
_____
○
_____
○
_____
○
_____
○
_____
○
_____

24 FRIDAY

○
_____
○
_____
○
_____
○
_____
○
_____

July
2026

25 SATURDAY

-
-
-
-
-
-
-
-

26 SUNDAY

-
-
-
-
-
-
-
-

27 MONDAY

-
-
-
-
-
-
-
-

28 TUESDAY

-
-
-
-
-

29 WEDNESDAY

30 THURSDAY

31 FRIDAY

NOTES

August
2026

01 SATURDAY

- ○ _____
- ○ _____
- ○ _____
- ○ _____
- ○ _____
- ○ _____
- ○ _____
- ○ _____

02 SUNDAY

- ○ _____
- ○ _____
- ○ _____
- ○ _____
- ○ _____
- ○ _____
- ○ _____
- ○ _____

03 MONDAY

- ○ _____
- ○ _____
- ○ _____
- ○ _____
- ○ _____
- ○ _____
- ○ _____
- ○ _____

04 TUESDAY

- ○ _____
- ○ _____
- ○ _____
- ○ _____
- ○ _____

August
2026

05 WEDNESDAY

06 THURSDAY

07 FRIDAY

08 SATURDAY

August
2026

09 SUNDAY

○ _____
○ _____
○ _____
○ _____
○ _____
○ _____
○ _____
○ _____

10 MONDAY

○ _____
○ _____
○ _____
○ _____
○ _____
○ _____
○ _____
○ _____

11 TUESDAY

○ _____
○ _____
○ _____
○ _____
○ _____
○ _____
○ _____
○ _____

12 WEDNESDAY

○ _____
○ _____
○ _____
○ _____
○ _____

13 THURSDAY

14 FRIDAY

15 SATURDAY

16 SUNDAY

August
2026

17 MONDAY

○ _____
○ _____
○ _____
○ _____
○ _____
○ _____
○ _____
○ _____

18 TUESDAY

○ _____
○ _____
○ _____
○ _____
○ _____
○ _____
○ _____
○ _____

19 WEDNESDAY

○ _____
○ _____
○ _____
○ _____
○ _____
○ _____
○ _____

20 THURSDAY

○ _____
○ _____
○ _____
○ _____
○ _____

21 FRIDAY

22 SATURDAY

23 SUNDAY

24 MONDAY

August
2026

25 TUESDAY

○ _____
○ _____
○ _____
○ _____
○ _____
○ _____
○ _____
○ _____

26 WEDNESDAY

○ _____
○ _____
○ _____
○ _____
○ _____
○ _____
○ _____
○ _____

27 THURSDAY

○ _____
○ _____
○ _____
○ _____
○ _____
○ _____
○ _____
○ _____

28 FRIDAY

○ _____
○ _____
○ _____
○ _____
○ _____

August
2026

29 SATURDAY

○ _____
○ _____
○ _____
○ _____
○ _____
○ _____
○ _____
○ _____

30 SUNDAY

○ _____
○ _____
○ _____
○ _____
○ _____
○ _____
○ _____
○ _____

31 MONDAY

○ _____
○ _____
○ _____
○ _____
○ _____
○ _____
○ _____
○ _____

NOTES

_____
_____
_____
_____

September
2026

01 TUESDAY

○ _____
○ _____
○ _____
○ _____
○ _____
○ _____
○ _____
○ _____

02 WEDNESDAY

○ _____
○ _____
○ _____
○ _____
○ _____
○ _____
○ _____
○ _____

03 THURSDAY

○ _____
○ _____
○ _____
○ _____
○ _____
○ _____
○ _____
○ _____

04 FRIDAY

○ _____
○ _____
○ _____
○ _____
○ _____

05 SATURDAY

○
○
○
○
○
○
○
○

06 SUNDAY

○
○
○
○
○
○
○
○

07 MONDAY

○
○
○
○
○
○
○
○

08 TUESDAY

○
○
○
○
○

09 WEDNESDAY

○
○
○
○
○
○
○
○

10 THURSDAY

○
○
○
○
○
○
○
○

11 FRIDAY

○
○
○
○
○
○
○
○

12 SATURDAY

○
○
○
○
○

13 SUNDAY

○ _____
○ _____
○ _____
○ _____
○ _____
○ _____
○ _____
○ _____

14 MONDAY

○ _____
○ _____
○ _____
○ _____
○ _____
○ _____
○ _____
○ _____

15 TUESDAY

○ _____
○ _____
○ _____
○ _____
○ _____
○ _____
○ _____
○ _____

16 WEDNESDAY

○ _____
○ _____
○ _____
○ _____

17 THURSDAY

○ _____
○ _____
○ _____
○ _____
○ _____
○ _____
○ _____
○ _____

18 FRIDAY

○ _____
○ _____
○ _____
○ _____
○ _____
○ _____
○ _____
○ _____

19 SATURDAY

○ _____
○ _____
○ _____
○ _____
○ _____
○ _____
○ _____
○ _____

20 SUNDAY

○ _____
○ _____
○ _____
○ _____
○ _____

21 MONDAY

○ _____
○ _____
○ _____
○ _____
○ _____
○ _____
○ _____
○ _____

22 TUESDAY

○ _____
○ _____
○ _____
○ _____
○ _____
○ _____
○ _____
○ _____

23 WEDNESDAY

○ _____
○ _____
○ _____
○ _____
○ _____
○ _____
○ _____
○ _____

24 THURSDAY

○ _____
○ _____
○ _____
○ _____
○ _____

September
2026

25 FRIDAY

○ _____
○ _____
○ _____
○ _____
○ _____
○ _____
○ _____
○ _____

26 SATURDAY

○ _____
○ _____
○ _____
○ _____
○ _____
○ _____
○ _____
○ _____

27 SUNDAY

○ _____
○ _____
○ _____
○ _____
○ _____
○ _____
○ _____
○ _____

28 MONDAY

○ _____
○ _____
○ _____
○ _____
○ _____

29 TUESDAY

- ○
- ○
- ○
- ○
- ○
- ○
- ○
- ○

30 WEDNESDAY

- ○
- ○
- ○
- ○
- ○
- ○
- ○
- ○

NOTES

October
2026

01 THURSDAY
-
-
-
-
-
-
-
-

02 FRIDAY
-
-
-
-
-
-
-
-

03 SATURDAY
-
-
-
-
-
-
-
-

04 SUNDAY
-
-
-
-
-

October
2026

05 MONDAY

○
○
○
○
○
○
○
○

06 TUESDAY

○
○
○
○
○
○
○
○

07 WEDNESDAY

○
○
○
○
○
○
○
○

08 THURSDAY

○
○
○
○
○

October
2026

09 FRIDAY
○ _____
○ _____
○ _____
○ _____
○ _____
○ _____
○ _____
○ _____

10 SATURDAY
○ _____
○ _____
○ _____
○ _____
○ _____
○ _____
○ _____
○ _____

11 SUNDAY
○ _____
○ _____
○ _____
○ _____
○ _____
○ _____
○ _____
○ _____

12 MONDAY
○ _____
○ _____
○ _____
○ _____
○ _____

13 TUESDAY

14 WEDNESDAY

15 THURSDAY

16 FRIDAY

October
2026

17 SATURDAY
○
○
○
○
○
○
○
○

18 SUNDAY
○
○
○
○
○
○
○
○

19 MONDAY
○
○
○
○
○
○
○
○

20 TUESDAY
○
○
○
○
○

October
2026

21 WEDNESDAY

22 THURSDAY

23 FRIDAY

24 SATURDAY

October
2026

25 SUNDAY

○ _____
○ _____
○ _____
○ _____
○ _____
○ _____
○ _____
○ _____

26 MONDAY

○ _____
○ _____
○ _____
○ _____
○ _____
○ _____
○ _____
○ _____

27 TUESDAY

○ _____
○ _____
○ _____
○ _____
○ _____
○ _____
○ _____
○ _____

28 WEDNESDAY

○ _____
○ _____
○ _____
○ _____
○ _____

October
2026

29 THURSDAY
○ _____
○ _____
○ _____
○ _____
○ _____
○ _____
○ _____
○ _____

30 FRIDAY
○ _____
○ _____
○ _____
○ _____
○ _____
○ _____
○ _____
○ _____

31 SATURDAY
○ _____
○ _____
○ _____
○ _____
○ _____
○ _____
○ _____

NOTES
_____
_____
_____
_____

November
2026

01 SUNDAY

○ _____
○ _____
○ _____
○ _____
○ _____
○ _____
○ _____
○ _____

02 MONDAY

○ _____
○ _____
○ _____
○ _____
○ _____
○ _____
○ _____
○ _____

03 TUESDAY

○ _____
○ _____
○ _____
○ _____
○ _____
○ _____
○ _____
○ _____

04 WEDNESDAY

○ _____
○ _____
○ _____
○ _____
○ _____

November
2026

05 THURSDAY

06 FRIDAY

07 SATURDAY

08 SUNDAY

November
2026

09 MONDAY

○
○
○
○
○
○
○
○

10 TUESDAY

○
○
○
○
○
○
○
○

11 WEDNESDAY

○
○
○
○
○
○
○
○

12 THURSDAY

○
○
○
○
○

13 FRIDAY

○
○
○
○
○
○
○
○

14 SATURDAY

○
○
○
○
○
○
○
○

15 SUNDAY

○
○
○
○
○
○
○
○

16 MONDAY

○
○
○
○
○

November
2026

17 TUESDAY

○ _____
○ _____
○ _____
○ _____
○ _____
○ _____
○ _____
○ _____

18 WEDNESDAY

○ _____
○ _____
○ _____
○ _____
○ _____
○ _____
○ _____
○ _____

19 THURSDAY

○ _____
○ _____
○ _____
○ _____
○ _____
○ _____
○ _____
○ _____

20 FRIDAY

○ _____
○ _____
○ _____
○ _____
○ _____

November
2026

21 SATURDAY
○
○
○
○
○
○
○

22 SUNDAY
○
○
○
○
○
○
○
○

23 MONDAY
○
○
○
○
○
○
○
○

24 TUESDAY
○
○
○
○
○

November
2026

25 WEDNESDAY

○ _____
○ _____
○ _____
○ _____
○ _____
○ _____
○ _____
○ _____

26 THURSDAY

○ _____
○ _____
○ _____
○ _____
○ _____
○ _____
○ _____
○ _____

27 FRIDAY

○ _____
○ _____
○ _____
○ _____
○ _____
○ _____
○ _____
○ _____

28 SATURDAY

○ _____
○ _____
○ _____
○ _____
○ _____

November
2026

29 SUNDAY

- ◯ _____
- ◯ _____
- ◯ _____
- ◯ _____
- ◯ _____
- ◯ _____
- ◯ _____
- ◯ _____

30 MONDAY

- ◯ _____
- ◯ _____
- ◯ _____
- ◯ _____
- ◯ _____
- ◯ _____
- ◯ _____
- ◯ _____

NOTES

_____
_____
_____
_____
_____
_____
_____
_____
_____
_____
_____

December
2026

01 TUESDAY

○ _____
○ _____
○ _____
○ _____
○ _____
○ _____
○ _____
○ _____

02 WEDNESDAY

○ _____
○ _____
○ _____
○ _____
○ _____
○ _____
○ _____
○ _____

03 THURSDAY

○ _____
○ _____
○ _____
○ _____
○ _____
○ _____
○ _____
○ _____

04 FRIDAY

○ _____
○ _____
○ _____
○ _____
○ _____

December
2026

05 SATURDAY

06 SUNDAY

07 MONDAY

08 TUESDAY

09 WEDNESDAY

○ _____
○ _____
○ _____
○ _____
○ _____
○ _____
○ _____
○ _____

10 THURSDAY

○ _____
○ _____
○ _____
○ _____
○ _____
○ _____
○ _____
○ _____

11 FRIDAY

○ _____
○ _____
○ _____
○ _____
○ _____
○ _____
○ _____
○ _____

12 SATURDAY

○ _____
○ _____
○ _____
○ _____
○ _____

December
2026

13 SUNDAY

14 MONDAY

15 TUESDAY

16 WEDNESDAY

17 THURSDAY

○
○
○
○
○
○
○
○

18 FRIDAY

○
○
○
○
○
○
○
○

19 SATURDAY

○
○
○
○
○
○
○
○

20 SUNDAY

○
○
○
○
○

21 MONDAY

22 TUESDAY

23 WEDNESDAY

24 THURSDAY

25 FRIDAY

○ _____
○ _____
○ _____
○ _____
○ _____
○ _____
○ _____
○ _____

26 SATURDAY

○ _____
○ _____
○ _____
○ _____
○ _____
○ _____
○ _____
○ _____

27 SUNDAY

○ _____
○ _____
○ _____
○ _____
○ _____
○ _____
○ _____
○ _____

28 MONDAY

○ _____
○ _____
○ _____
○ _____
○ _____

December
2026

29 TUESDAY

○ _____
○ _____
○ _____
○ _____
○ _____
○ _____
○ _____
○ _____

30 WEDNESDAY

○ _____
○ _____
○ _____
○ _____
○ _____
○ _____
○ _____
○ _____

31 THURSDAY

○ _____
○ _____
○ _____
○ _____
○ _____
○ _____
○ _____
○ _____

NOTES

_____
_____
_____
_____

www.ingramcontent.com/pod-product-compliance
Lightning Source LLC
Chambersburg PA
CBHW081333120626

46546CB00011B/3331